ANIMALS
and Their Mates

HOW ANIMALS ATTRACT, FIGHT FOR AND PROTECT EACH OTHER

WRITTEN BY PAMELA HICKMAN
ILLUSTRATED BY PAT STEPHENS

Kids Can Press

12/04

WI

...acey Roderick, Pat Stephens, Marie Bartholomew
and the rest of the wonderful Kids Can Press staff.

For Doug — PH
To my mother — PS

Kids Can Press acknowledges the financial support of the Government of Ontario, through the Ontario Media Development Corporation's Ontario Book Initiative; the Ontario Arts Council; the Canada Council for the Arts; and the Government of Canada, through the BPIDP, for our publishing activity.

Published in Canada by
Kids Can Press Ltd.
29 Birch Avenue
Toronto, ON M4V 1E2

Published in the U.S. by
Kids Can Press Ltd.
2250 Military Road
Tonawanda, NY 14150

www.kidscanpress.com

Edited by Stacey Roderick
Designed by Marie Bartholomew
Printed in Hong Kong, China, by Book Art Inc., Toronto

The hardcover edition of this book is smyth sewn casebound.

The paperback edition of this book is limp sewn with a drawn-on cover.

CM 04   0 9 8 7 6 5 4 3 2 1
CM PA 04   0 9 8 7 6 5 4 3 2 1

National Library of Canada Cataloguing in Publication Data

Hickman, Pamela
    Animals and their mates : how animals attract, fight for and protect each other / written by Pamela Hickman ; illustrated by Pat Stephens.

Includes index.
ISBN 1-55337-545-9 (bound).
ISBN 1-55337-546-7 (pbk.)

1. Courtship of animals — Juvenile literature.
2. Sexual behavior in animals — Juvenile literature. I. Stephens, Pat II. Title.

QL751.5.H53 2004   j591.56'2
C2003-905442-X

Kids Can Press is a l©rus™ Entertainment company

Contents

Introduction

A nest of fluffy chicks, a litter of furry baby rabbits and a pond full of tiny tadpoles are all signs that animals have been mating. All animals are born with the instinct, or need, to mate. Mating is the way animals produce more of their own kind and pass on their genes, or special characteristics, to the next generation. Genes decide things like an animal's color and size.

The female's body produces egg cells that contain her genes, and the male produces sperm cells that contain his. During mating, a sperm cell must fertilize, or join together with, an egg cell to begin growing into a baby. Depending on the species, fertilization takes place either inside the female's body or outside.

You may think screaming, fighting and urinating in public is rude, but some animals do these things to attract and win mates. There are animals that mate for life, others that spend only minutes with their mate and some that die right after mating. Discover why mice mate when they are only a few months old and why grizzly bears wait for years before they mate. Find out how an orangutan finds a partner in its huge territory and why an osprey never has to search for one. From brilliantly colored birds to slimy slugs and smelly seals, you'll learn how and where animals mate, and much more!

Anole lizards

Attracting a mate

What do a firefly's light, a spring peeper frog's song, a giraffe's nuzzle and a camel's scent have in common? They are all ways animals signal they are looking for a mate. In many species, the females are in charge of choosing a mate. They pick the males that are most attractive to their senses of sight, hearing, smell, taste or touch. These male greater birds of paradise attract females with their special, showy feathers.

If you were a male greater bird of paradise ...

- you would grow long, brightly colored feathers for the mating season.
- you and other males would clear the leaves from a branch at the top of a tree to perform a mating song and dance to attract females.
- you would quickly mate with the first female that flew up to you. After mating, she would fly away to nest and raise her young alone.
- you would mate with many females over several months.
- you would shed your special feathers when mating season ended.

Dazzling displays

People sometimes dress in bright colors and fancy clothes to attract attention. Many animals have similar ways of getting noticed. Male anole lizards have a brightly colored throat pouch they puff out to attract females and warn other males to stay away. Male warblers grow colorful feathers to attract females during the spring mating season. Once breeding is over, the males molt, or shed, their special feathers and grow duller-colored ones.

Tropical butterfly fish can change their colors much more easily. Special color cells in their skin change in response to their behavior. When males prepare to breed, they are excited and aggressive. Their colors become brighter and change pattern, and they raise their fins to appear larger and stronger. Once mating is over, their usual colors and pattern return.

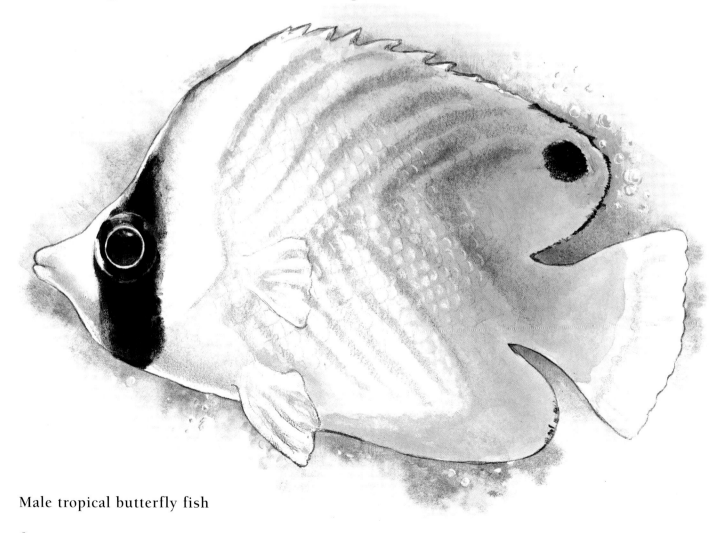

Male tropical butterfly fish

Male yellow warbler

Over here!

Male jumping spiders and wolf spiders are smaller than the females, who can mistake them for food. The males wave and vibrate their brightly colored palps, which are like mini front legs, in a certain way to send the message that they are ready to mate.

Sometimes looking good isn't enough. Many males have to perform for their mates. They may have a special walk, like a whooping crane, or do twirls and dives in the air, like a woodcock or common tern.

Male fireflies light up the night as they fly around and flash their lights at nearby females. Each firefly species has its own special light pattern, like a code. If a female of the same species is ready to mate, she flashes back the same code from her resting place on the ground. The first male to reach her becomes her mate.

Male jumping spider

Sounding off

Making noise is a good way to get attention. That is why most wildlife make noise when they are attracting and competing for mates.

Have you ever woken up early to birds' songs? In the tropics you could wake to a chorus of monkeys. Scientists believe male animals sing early in the morning after a chilly night with no food to display their fitness to females—and to male competition. Since singing requires a lot of energy, females choose the best singers as the healthiest mates.

Male howler monkeys

Nature's noisemakers

Animals use a variety of body parts to make themselves heard when they are ready to mate. Check out these male noisemakers.

Crabs and lobsters snap their large claws the way you might snap your fingers when you want someone's attention.

Toads and frogs inflate their throat sacs with air to produce a variety of calls, from trills to snores, depending on the species.

Ruffed grouse flap their wings quickly to create a deep drumming sound in the woods.

Crickets, grasshoppers and katydids use a combination of hind legs and wings rubbing together to make their familiar chirping sounds.

Smelly signals

Some people wear perfume or aftershave to be noticed. Wild animals also use smells to communicate with others, especially during mating season.

Many animals have scent glands that give off special smells, called pheromones, to attract a mate. Some creatures are so sensitive to pheromones that they can find a mate over long distances simply by sniffing. A male atlas moth, one of the biggest moths in the world, uses its large, feathery antennae to smell a mate up to 11 km (6.8 mi.) away!

Mammals have well-developed senses of smell and taste that are important during mating. For instance, when a female dog is in heat, or ready to mate, her body gives off a scent that male dogs smell kilometers (miles) away. Male seals give off a strong, musky odor in spring to signal to female seals that they are ready to mate. Male camels, horses and deer find out if a female is ready to mate by smelling and tasting her urine.

Male atlas moth

Wild about perfume?

The next time you pass the perfume counter in a store, stop and read some of the labels. The musk from cats, deer and, most expensively, whales are used in making some perfumes. Musk is a common animal sexual scent.

Tasty treats

A box of chocolates is a yummy treat from a special friend, but how would you like a ball of saliva or a paralyzed insect? Male scorpion flies attract mates with these tasty gifts. A male common tern may carry a fish in his beak while he performs a special mating flight. If the female seems interested, the male dives down and delivers the fish. To please a female limpkin, a kind of wading bird, a male offers her a snail removed from the shell. If she takes and eats the snail, she has chosen him as her mate. A male chimpanzee may share some meat with a female so she will accept him as a mate.

Scorpion fly mates

Male limpkin

Tern mates

The right touch

Animals may use touch to identify possible mates, as well as to show their intention to mate. Spiders that are active at night can't see each other, so they carefully rub each other's long legs when they meet. If everything feels right, they get closer in order to mate. Female web-spinning spiders can sense whether a mate or a victim has landed in their web by the way the threads vibrate. Male spiders pluck a certain part of the web in a precise way to make sure there is no confusion!

Once a partner is chosen, a special touch may still be necessary. Male and female giraffes rub necks and swing their heads back and forth before mating occurs. Porcupines approach each other on their hind feet, come together, place their paws on each other's shoulders and rub noses. They may also tumble and wrestle on the ground before mating.

Porcupine mates

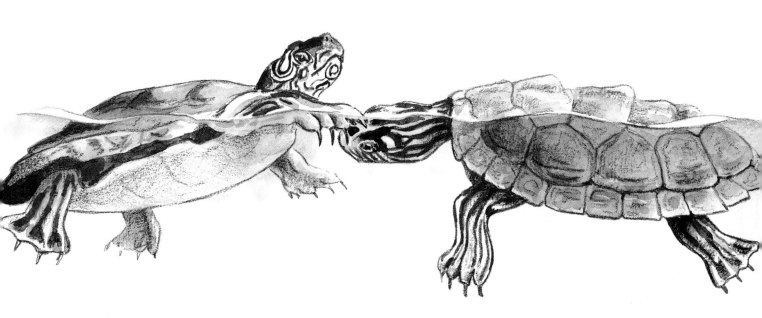

Gannet mates face each other, point their heads in the air and gently tap their bills together from side to side, as if they were fencing with swords.

Gannet mates

A male alligator moves in beside his chosen female for a few days before mating. He strokes her back with his front legs, rubs her throat with his head and even blows bubbles in the water near her cheeks. Male false map turtles use their clawed front feet to drum on the larger female's snout before they mate.

Even after mating, touch is the way some species send the message "We're still partners." American avocets walk together in shallow water with their bills crossed and one of the male bird's wings over the female's back after they've mated.

False map turtle mates

Joining the crowd

Finding a mate is easier when animals get together in large groups. When lots of males and females are in one area, getting a mate takes less time and less energy. Penguins gather in huge colonies, or large groups, each spring to mate and nest side by side with thousands of other pairs. Eels migrate, or travel, hundreds of kilometers (miles) to meet other eels for breeding.

These red-sided garter snakes crowd together in caves and rock crevices each fall to hibernate, when their body temperature lowers and breathing rate slows way down for the winter. In spring, they don't have to go anywhere to find mates.

If you were a female red-sided garter snake …

- males would leave the cave first after hibernating and wait for you outside.
- you would give off a special scent so a male could tell you were a female, since males and females look alike.
- you would become part of a huge tangle of males fighting over females.
- you would leave to find food as soon as you mated.
- you would give birth alone to about 40 live babies (not eggs).

Getting together

You may have heard there is safety in numbers. There are also more possible mates.

Many birds, such as gulls and puffins, breed in colonies. Chinstrap penguins have the largest colony of all, with five million mating pairs on the South Sandwich Islands!

Scientists have found that seabirds living in large colonies seem to respond to "peer pressure." Being surrounded by thousands of other birds mating and laying eggs seems to drive birds to keep up with the crowd, so they mate more often and lay their eggs sooner than seabirds living in smaller groups.

Some insects form mating swarms immediately after hatching. Large groups of flying ants contain hundreds or thousands of mating pairs. Male mayflies hatch first and form swarms over a stream as they wait for the females to hatch. As soon as a female enters the swarm, she is carried off by a male for mating.

Humpback whales find their mates when they gather annually in large groups to migrate, or move, northward to their summer feeding grounds in the northern Atlantic and Pacific oceans.

Mayflies

Chinstrap penguins

Huge numbers of freshwater turtles in South America migrate long distances down rivers at the beginning of their breeding season. Once they reach their sandy breeding beaches, they mate and lay their eggs all at once. Each year, thousands of adult sockeye salmon leave the ocean to return to the rivers where they hatched. Once there, the males fight each other for a mating space. The winners are then joined by their female partners. After mating, the exhausted couple dies and their eggs hatch on their own.

Freshwater turtles

Fighting for rights

Getting or keeping a mate is key to the survival of an animal species because mating is the only way an animal can pass on its genes to the next generation. Since all animals need to mate, there can be competition for partners and some may have to fight for the right to mate. Females sometimes fight over mates, but in most species the males are the ones that do battle. Each mating season, male moose, like these ones, prepare to bash heads in order to claim a female.

If you were a male moose ...

- you would grow a new pair of antlers each year. The bigger your antlers, the more attractive you would be to a female.
- you would return to the same breeding grounds each fall to find a mate.
- you might have to fight with rival males. You would head butt your opponent and use your antlers to injure him. If you won, you would mate with the female.
- you would mate with several females during the rutting, or mating, season but each female would mate only once.
- your antlers would fall off after the rutting season ended.

Mighty males

Some male animals fight each other to win a mate. Since the strongest or healthiest male usually wins the fight, he is the one that mates and passes on his genes to the next generation. This helps to keep the population healthy.

Fighting is a last resort. Males prefer to scare off their competition by displaying their superior size or color or by making loud noises. Colorful male mandrills flash their sharp canine teeth at rival males.

Male mandrill

Northern elephant seal males, weighing up to 1800 kg (2 tons), have a trunklike inflatable nose sac. During mating season, they inflate it to warn away other males. They also defend their breeding territories by bellowing and, if that doesn't work, by fighting. Battling males face each other and rear up. They throw themselves forward and try to land on top of their opponent to crush him.

Male elephant seals

Fight to the finish

Occasionally, a head-bashing fight over females between Dall sheep, deer, moose or elk ends in death for both participants. Their horns or antlers can lock together. Caught in this position, the males cannot feed or defend themselves. Hikers sometimes find skulls of two animals with their antlers still tangled together long after death.

Male members of the goat and deer families use their horns or antlers to compete during breeding season. Often the male with the largest headgear wins without a fight. Sometimes, however, a pair of males run at each other, heads down, and smash their antlers or horns together in a show of strength. After several head butts, one of the opponents usually gives up and leaves.

Male lions sometimes fight to the death when a new male lion challenges the male leader of a pride of females. If the new male wins the fight, he may kill the pride's cubs so he can mate with the females and produce his own offspring.

Male lions

23

Female fighters

Jacana harem

In some species, females fight over mates, especially when males help feed and protect the young. Females compete for the best mates to ensure their young have the greatest chance of survival. A male that puts energy into raising young tends to be fussier about whom he mates with. He chooses the largest or most successful female—the one that wins the fight.

A jacana female has a harem, or group, of males who each raise a clutch of her eggs. The female fights other females for new males to add to her harem. She may even destroy another female's eggs and replace them with her own.

Male three-spined stickleback fish are excellent caretakers of their babies, so females fight over who gets the most watchful males.

When Mormon cricket females fight each other, there is more at stake than just a mate. Each male produces a sperm package to fertilize the female's eggs. The package also contains extra nutrients the female uses to make more eggs. Because it takes a huge amount of energy for the male to make his sperm package, he is very choosy about who gets it.

Female Mormon crickets

Mueller gibbon mates

Sometimes females drive other females out of their breeding territory in order to keep their mates to themselves. This is because females tend to have fewer young if a male has more than one mate at a time. Mueller gibbon pairs sing together to drive other pairs of gibbons from their territory. But if a single female stranger calls, the resident female chases off her competition.

Danger!

Mating can be deadly for some males. Male honeybees explode and die when they mate with a queen. Fierce female fireflies, biting midges, orb weaver spiders and mantids often eat their mates!

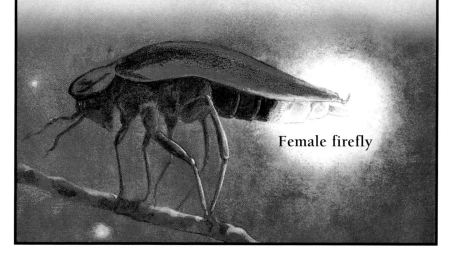

Female firefly

Perfect partners?

The number of mates an animal has and how long partners stay together depends on the species. Some animals, such as frogs, mate with many different partners each breeding season. Others, such as chipmunks, have one partner for the season but change partners each year. Pairs of tamarins (a kind of monkey) stay together for life, but deer separate right after mating.

This male orangutan lives alone in a huge territory that he defends from other males. One of his greatest challenges is finding a new partner each mating season.

If you were a male orangutan …

- you would mate only once a year.
- you would attract a female by calling, shaking branches and toppling over dead trees. You'd fill your huge throat pouch with air to make your calls louder so you could be heard over several kilometers (miles).
- your loudness would be a clue to how big you were. Females are most attracted to the loudest, and therefore biggest, mates.
- you would mate with the female that chose you and then leave her to raise the family. She would not mate again for eight or nine years.

Many mates

In general, the more babies an animal has, the more genes it will pass on to future generations. It is easier for a male to be a parent to more offspring than a female, especially for mammals. During mating, it takes the male anywhere from just a few minutes to several hours to contribute his sperm to make the babies. But afterward, the female spends weeks, months or possibly years growing the babies inside her, and then feeding and caring for them after birth.

Males of some species produce more young by mating with several females each breeding season. Deer and marten males mate with many females, but each female has only one mate and raises her family alone. Lion, marmot, zebra and gorilla males each have a harem of females that are lifelong mates. Male gray seals, pronghorns and woodland caribou collect different harems each breeding season.

Marmoset mates

Some mates, such as marmosets and bald eagles, stay in pairs for life. Since the male has only one mate, he has only a few offspring each year. Instead of spending his energy mating with many females, the male puts his effort into making his one pairing as successful as possible. His offspring have a much greater chance of surviving since he stays around to help feed and protect them.

Yellow-eyed penguins of New Zealand don't mate for life, but they may keep the same mates for up to 13 years. Macaroni penguin pairs usually stay together for four years in a row. Muskrats change mates each year but stay with their mate for the whole breeding season. Other animals, such as mountain lions and skunks, come together only to mate and then separate soon after. Both male and female porcupines, walruses and some bears mate several times with different partners each breeding season.

Marten mates

Unknown mates

Many sea creatures, such as jellyfish, release their eggs and sperm into the sea, where they mix at random to produce the next generation. Female frogs and fish lay their eggs in water, where they are fertilized by their mates. However, sometimes an intruding male sneaks in and adds his own sperm to the eggs.

Jellyfish

Mutual mates

Earthworms, snails and slugs are both male and female at the same time. This means every one produces both eggs and sperm. To reproduce, though, they must mate with another individual. So when two earthworms come together to mate, they exchange sperm and both lay eggs.

Earthworm mates

Mating time

When you think of animals mating and having babies, you usually think of spring. There are species that mate and give birth during winter, too, and some that breed year-round. In general, animals mate when it is easiest and give birth when the babies have the best chance of survival. Deer mate in the fall so the babies are born in spring when the weather is better and more food is available. Muskrat and least shrews that live in the north breed only in summer, but those that live in the south breed year-round because the weather is always warm and there is plenty of food.

Different species are ready to start mating at different ages, from a few months to many years old. Harbor seals are five or six years old before they begin to mate.

If you were a female harbor seal …

- you would join a large group of females at the same time and place each year to make it easier for the males to find you.
- you would mate once a year between July and September.
- you and the other pregnant females would give birth at the same time each year.
- your baby would be born in spring. After a month, your young would stop nursing, or drinking your milk, and begin finding its own food. You would then mate again.

Starting out

Grizzlies

Imagine if your mother gave birth to you when she was only a month old! That's what female deer mice do. But a female grizzly bear is six or seven years old before she is ready to mate. Once an animal reaches puberty, or its body is sexually mature and able to reproduce, it can mate and have babies.

The age of puberty varies greatly between species. In general, bigger species live longer and reach puberty at an older age. Animals with a short life span, such as mice, breed when they are very young so they can have as many babies as possible before they die.

When an animal can mate successfully to produce young depends on many things, including its age, the time of year, the climate and the amount of available nesting space and food. Muskrats reach puberty at six months if they live in a warm climate, but if they live where the winters are cold, they aren't sexually mature until they are a year old. Mating later prevents them from having babies when it is too cold and there is not enough food.

Muskrats

When there is lots of habitat for breeding and raising young, more animals mate and reproduce. If there are few breeding sites, older animals that already have territories mate first, and younger ones have to wait for another year or longer. Because fewer babies are born when food and shelter are scarce, more animals survive.

Sometimes female and male mammals within the same species reach puberty at different ages. Female musk oxen mate when they are three and a half years old, but males don't mate until they are five years old. Long-tailed weasel females reproduce when they are three or four months old but the males are a full year old before they are able to. Since it takes a relatively long time for a female mammal to grow a baby inside her body and raise it, starting at an earlier age gives her a chance to produce more offspring.

Musk oxen

Mating months

Some animals mate at specific times of year, while others have no special season for mating. For some, mating depends on other activities, such as hibernation or migration. In northern areas with long, cold winters, spring is when migrating birds return from the south and hibernating animals wake up. Soon after there seem to be baby animals everywhere.

Birds return in the spring because there is lots of space for nesting and plenty of food. They mate and raise their young in the spring and summer so that the young are big enough to fly south in the fall. Caribou mate during their fall migration and then give birth during their spring migration when the weather and food supply are better.

Some hibernators, such as frogs, snakes and woodchucks, mate in the spring when they come out of their winter homes. Their babies begin to develop right away. Bears mate in the summer, long before they begin their winter sleep alone. The growth of their embryos, or developing babies, does not begin right away. This is called delayed implantation. The babies start developing in late fall and are born in midwinter. This gives them time to nurse and grow for a couple of months before coming out of their den in the spring when the weather and food supply are better.

Caribou

Generally, once a female becomes pregnant she stops mating until she has given birth. The babies of small animals develop quickly so the adults can mate and give birth several times in a year. Lemmings give birth 23 days after mating, and then they mate again. The larger the animal, the longer the baby's gestation, or development, period. A female rhinoceros is pregnant for a year and a half before her baby is born and she won't mate again until the following year, when her baby needs less care.

Rhinoceroses

Winter babies

Most birds mate and nest in the spring, but the great horned owl is an exception. Adults find partners in the fall and mate in early winter. The eggs are laid in late January or early February, and the owlets hatch a month later, even though there may be snow on the ground.

Great horned owls

Mating spaces

There's no place like home. Most animals travel only as far as necessary from where they were raised to find a breeding place. Animals that migrate long distances, such as some birds, whales and fish, usually return to where they were raised to mate and have young. Bald eagles and osprey return to the same nests year after year with the same mates. Whether it's a nest, a small patch of ground or a large stretch of forest, most animals claim and fiercely defend their breeding territory from intruders, including people.

If you were a female osprey...

- you would migrate back to the area where you hatched and find a mate when you were three years old.
- you would choose your mate based on his special flying performance.
- you would have the same mate for life, although your mate might also have other partners.
- you and your mate would return to the same nest every spring. You would work on the nest together for several weeks or months, adding new sticks and a fresh lining.
- your mate would present you with a special stick or fish just before mating.
- your mate would feed and protect you while you hatched your eggs.

Special spots

You might meet your friends at school or the mall. Wild animals also have meeting places, particularly during mating season.

Red-eyed tree frogs mate 9 m (30 ft.) off the ground in trees in tropical jungles. When a male finds a female, he climbs onto her back and she carries him to a special place for mating — a leaf that overhangs some water. She lays her eggs on the leaf and he immediately fertilizes them with his sperm. Within a couple of days, the tiny tadpoles hatch and drop into the water below where they develop into frogs.

In some cases, males build a special place to attract and court females. The male Australian magpie goose builds a platform of grasses in a marsh where he shows off for nearby females. Once he has attracted one or two females for mating, they work together to build a nest on top of his original structure and raise their families there.

Three-spined stickleback fish also construct special spots for mating. The male fish builds a tunnel-like nest on the bottom of a river or lake and then finds females to bring to it. The female follows the male to the nest but swims into the tunnel first. Inside, she lays some of her eggs while the male follows her and fertilizes them. When she is finished, she swims away to mate with other males. The nest builder attracts other females to lay their eggs inside his nest, too. Once there are several hundred eggs in his nest, the male looks after them and cares for the young.

Red-eyed tree frog mates

Australian magpie geese

Three-spined stickleback mates

A slimy spot

Great gray slugs meet on branches
and circle each other for over an hour
before mating. Once they are ready to
mate, they produce lots of slime from
special glands. Together they hang
from the branch on a rope of slime and
mate for up to 24 hours.

Great gray slug mates

Index